FOR WOMEN MONOLOGUES THEY HAVEN'T HEARD

Susan Pomerance

FOR WOMEN, MONOLOGUES THEY HAVEN'T HEARD:

How many times have you needed a fresh, contemporary, relevant speech to deliver and have had to resort to a tired war-horse? And how about those all important auditions? Face it, casting directors are bored stiff sitting through those "proven" monologues that bore them to tears and are counter-productive to your goals.

This collection contains new speeches written in real speech for today's actress. They are ideal for your special readings, class work, workshops and auditions.

For information write: Dramaline Publications, Publisher, 10470 Riverside Drive, Suite #201, Toluca Lake, CA 91602.

CONTENTS

III

COMEDY

MEDEDITH

Meredith reveals her disgust for the singles scene.

The "Happy Hour?" Are they kidding? If it's all so damned gloriously happy how come the people are never smiling? I ask you, Ruth, why? I never see any happiness. Unless you call brassy, unemotional laughter happiness.

Usually what you find is this bunch of really lonely, loaded people who are very *very* serious about sex; determined to make it with somebody, anybody. It's seek and destroy in these places. "Happy?" Are they kidding? It's all more tragic than anything else.

Like last week, when you and I stopped by Clancy's, you know? How about that? All those overdressed yuppies getting smashed. I mean, I may be looking, but not for that, not for any of those turkeys. And the nerve they have trying to con you into believing they're interested in a "meaningful" relationship. You talk about your raging arrogance. The only relationship they're interested in is a quickie in the back of their BMW.

Besides, who in their right mind would make it with a total stranger these days? With the stuff that's floating around out there? Hey! Junior execs in Porches and clean shirts are one thing — private parts are another. Before I go making it with anyone today I wanna see his latest medical records, okay?

No, Ruth, the so called "happy hour," the juvenile behavior, the cheap-o well drinks and stale snacks aren't for me. In fact, I actually find the whole scene disgusting — perverse. If I meet someone it's not going to be in some meat market where the mentality is a dense as the cigarette smoke.

Goodbye Norma Jean
Though I never knew you at all
You had the grace to hold yourself
While those around you crawled.
They crawled out of the woodwork
And they whispered into your brain
Set you on the treadmill
And made you change your name.

Bernie Taupin. British songwriter. From the song:
"Candle in the Wind."

CAROL

She covers the travails of divorce.

You decide to call it quits and you shake hands on it and everything seems to be rational and sane. You discuss dividing the property like adults; you help him pack and there's no animosity and you're both relieved and wonder why the hell you didn't end the whole thing months ago. Then — then you get lawyers and everything changes. Things get serious.

And things get *really* serious when you realize there's over nine hundred thousand involved. Or, should I say, after the *lawyers* realize there's over nine hundred thousand involved. Then you get into the proposals and counter proposals. And your original list is scrutinized and contested because you forgot to list the signed china pieces and other valuable goodies. Anyway, little things crop up and questions are raised and suspicion creeps in. Now, why does he want that old cedar chest? He didn't at first. Could the damned thing be priceless? Maybe a secret panel with cash?

Then your lawyer starts calling every day. And he talks very calmly and slowly. For two hundred bucks an hour he loves to be calm and slow. And then, someone makes a ridiculous demand. Like one of you comes up with something like keeping the

5

house in exchange for the garden tools, something wild like that. And then it hits the fan and gets ugly and names are called and everybody hates everybody. When we started out, everything was settled, more or less, you know? Now — it's war!

The divorce process, the whole thing is a real mess. It breaks you emotionally and financially and your often wind up mistrusting and hating someone you'd merely become incompatable with.

And oh yes, I ran into my attorney yesterday. The slow talking bastard was driving a new Mercedes.

It had only one fault. It was kind of lousy.
James Thurber (1894-1961). Remark made about a play.

FRANCES

Frances recommends homicide as retribution for blatant promiscuity.

There's only one thing to do. Murder him! *(Beat.)* No, I'm not crazy. It's the only way to defend your honor. You can't sit idly by and let him humiliate you like this. You're becoming a laughing stock. Face it, you've got an asshole for a husband. He doesn't give a damn about you or your feelings one way or other. Ted's a loser, a creep — face it. *(Beat for response.)*

Nonsense. Women knock off weasels like him all the time on the Alfred Hitchcock reruns on channel 12. They do these neat things with blunt instruments and poison and stuff. It's beautiful. Wow.

Do you realize your household's a regular gold mine of potential weapons? Like your kitchen knives, for instance. Or your garbage disposal — with the accent on "disposal." And like your gas. Gas is silent, subtle, clean and easy. You put in a batch of brownies, okay? And you suddenly remember you're out of something and you have to run down to the store, right? Hey, how did you know the pilot light was on the fritz? Perfect. The cops wouldn't have a clue. Also electricity. You just jimmy the 220 outlet to your dryer and when Ted checks it out,

he checks out. Instant potato chip, just like that!
And what about your pool? A natural. Ted would
go down like a brick with all that Budweiser in him.
Jan, you've got to get creatively vindictive and take
action before you become the laughing stock of
Riverdale. You can't stand by while Ted's out
making it with every woman in the county. You've
got to act.

Lemme ask you. Does he have plenty of insurance?
*(Beat for Jan's response. Then she rubs her hands
with glee.)* Oh, goody!

---

*One of Edward's Mistresses was Jane Shore, who has
had a play written about her, but it is a tragedy and
therefore not worth reading.* Jane Austin (1775-1817).

YVONNE

She knows that looks are a poor criteria for judging heterosexuality.

C'mon. I mean, how was I supposed to know? How would anyone? What about you? you met him.

What impressed me most about him initially was how uncomplicated and well-adjusted he was. No phoney baloney, no sunglasses in his hair, no cutsie lines like ninety percent of the men you meet. He seemed to be this normal, gentlemanly person who helped me pick up a dozen cans of cat food when my shopping bad bursted. He didn't come on, didn't push, nothing. He was just as helpful as could be and had this nice, relaxed way about him that you just had to find attractive, you know?

And here we'd lived together for almost a year, too. It as perfect. I mean, c'mon, let's face it, I've had other roommates. Larry seemed ideal. He was neat, kind, considerate. And he was a fantastic lover. It was heaven. I figured this was it, that my searching days were over. After a series of cesspools I'd finally discovered a virgin spring, right? Wrong.

He started getting these phone calls from this guy almost every day — a close friend, he said. At first, I didn't give it much thought. But, after awhile, I

9

started to get suspicious because Larry never asked him over. I mean, if they were such close friends wouldn't Larry want me to meet him? Wouldn't he ask him to drop by?

Then I saw them together. By accident one day. I was feeling rotten and I'd taken off early from work. Here they were, the two of them, walking down the sidewalk. I got the picture right away in glowing magenta. The guy was very mincy. And Larry was looking at him like he was strawberry pie. When I pressed him on it that evening he admitted he was bi. Nice, huh? I mean like, hey! I'm pretty broad minded but this I don't need. So — that ended it.

You just never know anymore these days. Some of the strongest looking packages are held together by pink ribbon.

She ran the whole gamut of the emotions from A to B. Dorothy Parker (1893-1967) US writer. Referring to a performance by Katharine Hepburn.

JAN

Jan relates her computer dating experiences.

I figured, what do I have to lose? I mean, after the terrible luck I'd had with regular dating, why not? And computer dating at least seemed to be a scientific approach.

The first thing they have you do is complete this mile long form loaded with personal questions. Then they do an up-close-and-personal video tape on you and then run your data through their flies and match you up with one of their clients. You know, someone in your sexual, social, and psychic ballpark.

My first matchup was with a distinguished looking man who was vice president of an accounting firm. He looked beautiful. So, they arranged a date. Well, let me tell you, he turned out to be nothing like his tape. He must have used a stand-in. The man was at least seventy-five and he was wearing a toupee that looked like a sick muskrat. And he was farsighted and kept knocking his Chablis into my Veal Oscar. And when the bill came he insisted on splitting it because it was the "liberated" thing to do.

The second guy I selected looked fantastic. Very masculine and outdoorsy like the men on cigarette billboards. But in the flesh he couldn't have been more than five feet tall. At dinner I was tempted to ask for a booster seat. I was a disaster of an evening. His data sheet stated he was a lab technician. Turned out he was an embalmers assistant. I coulnd't keep my eyes off his fingers and I almost threw up when he ripped apart his chicken.

I've had it with the computer dating bit. I'll take my chances in the supermarket checkout line. At least there, what you see it what you get — sort of.

> *In the theatre the audience want to be suprised — but by things that they expect.*
> Tristan Bernard (1866-1947) French dramatist.

JANICE

Janice is awakened to the fact that the boy next door is no longer just the boy next door.

How in the world could you ever predict something like this? It's...I mean, you're so close. We've been neighbors forever, since we were little kids. Playing together, messing around and stuff. I've always thought of Ralph Merriweather as this little playmate next door, you know? This goofy kid with unruly hair and a squeaky voice and acne. How in the hell was I to know I'd fall for Ralph Merriweather?

Things change, you know? One day here's this skinny, uncoordinated guy with a big Adam's apple and then, all of a sudden, you turn around and he's super-neat. One day he's a dork, the next — a hunk.

It happened last night when we went over to the Merriweather's for the holidays like we have since I can remember. Of course, there was mistletoe. And Ralph grabs me and kisses me, and — wow! All of a sudden like he's not just the little dork next door anymore. He's like this familiar stranger who turns me on. Amazing. After all these years. And now everything is turned upside down. Now I find him handsome and sexy and *very* interesting. Why, when we were little, we used to take baths together and I never ever once thought about looking below the water line. Hell, I was more interested in his plastic duck.

CLAUDIA

She rails against aging.

Certainly I hate the thought of it! You think there's some redeeming quality about aging? about the so called "golden years?" Please. Old age isn't golden, it's brass; it's dry skin and lusterless hair and buying the twenty gallon vat of Oil of Olay; it's two hours a day trying to conceal lines and wrinkles and sags and bags; it's when your center of gravity slips below your knees; it's when the latest fashions make you look like a court jester; it's diets and sugar substitute and avoiding *anything* with flavor; it's a major appliance Christmas; it's sensible shoes; it's getting calves as sore as boils from walking more than a city block; it's faking seeing what's on menus because it's impossible to see the damned things under three feet; it's getting invitations to class reunions and going and feeling like your in the middle of the elephants' burial ground; it's taking the elevator to the second floor; it's never bending over from the waist because your fifth lumbar goes out more often than you do; it's forgetting to remember not to take calls from people you're trying to forget; it's sticking your tongue out at a "Happiness Is Being A Grandparent" bumper sticker and realizing it's on *your* car; it's when the remote control switch becomes the most important thing about TV; it's when the two most vital liquids in your life are toner and dye; it's little

14

aches and pains and brown splotches and missing the eleven o'clock news because you're sound asleep in your chair.

Show me a woman who says she doesn't care about aging and getting wrinkles and losing her shape and becoming a dried up hunk of fruit that no man wants to pick I'll show you a liar. Aging is terrible. Aging is bullshit!

The play was a great success, but the audience was a disaster. Oscar Wilde (1854-1900).

LORNA

Lorna was a child prodigy, has an IQ of 170. Her superior intelligence, however, has offtimes proved problematical.

When I was three, I could hammer out little tunes on the piano and by five I was playing sonatas and fuges. I was giving recitals by the time I was nine. And math was never a problem, anything that required reasoning. I was into algebra and calculus at a very early age and could run answers down in my head before my teachers figured them out on calculators. It was the same with history — places and dates — I had total recall. I still do.

My childhood was kind of ridiculous. Here I was, this little kid, standing around intellectualizing while other children my age were out having a good time. While other girls my age were playing doctor, I was playing Brahms. And because of it, I was never a part of the "in" group, I was an outsider. Intellectual pursuits cut you out of the main stream and you get branded a "smarty pants." It wasn't easy.

To say my life's been an anomaly is a whopping understatement. A lot of the time I feel like some freak of nature, or something. People relate to me strangely, at arm's length, gingerly, like I'm this piece of fine china. And my relationships with men? Forget it. One sure way to mess it up with most men

16

is to show superior intelligence. And with me it's overkill. I can't keep from shooting off my smart fucking mouth.

It would be great to be below average intelligence; to know nothing; to be able to sit through Hamlet without mouthing all the parts; to be able to enjoy simple pursuits. What was it Sophocles said? "The happiest life consists in ignorance, before you learn to grieve and rejoice." Oh no! See — see there, I just did it again.

The weasel under the cocktail caabinet. Harold Pinter (1930-) Reply when asked what his plays were about.

ANNA

Anna has the inside track on Doris Lehman's meteoric rise within the firm.

You really wanna know how she's gotten there? Well, I'll tell you real quick how she's gotten there. She's *screwed* her way to the top, that's how. She's made it with everyone from the stock boy to the chairman. In fact, just between you and me, at the convention in Cincinnati last Fall, ya know? — Joe Easton saw her sneaking into the president's suite. The sly old boy nailed her at the Hilton.

There must be at least twenty guys in this company who've balled her. They pass her around like chip dip. How do you think she got upstairs so quickly? Brains? Do me a favor. She's lame. But if you allow yourself to be on bottom often enough — if you know what I mean — you're going to make it to the top. And Doris Lehman would do it with a garden hose at half time at the Super Bowl if she thought it would do her some good.

Sometimes I think it doesn't pay to be straight. Like me. What's being straight arrow gotten me? Zilch, that's what. Here I am, stuck down here in the typing pool with an antique IBM and a low-tech salary. And Lehman? Here she is making a bundle upstairs. And have you seen her office? An abstract

1 8

desk, computer, fancy phones, three windows overlooking the river, signed prints on the walls, and this steno chair from outer space.

And the couch in her boss' office? — a hide-a-bed. *(Beat.)* Nope, I'm not kidding. One of the janitorial guys told me. The thing opens out and right away you've got instant motel. And knowing Doris it probably has a built-in vibrator. The ambitious little trap's screwing the balls off Ralph Humble, you can bet on it. Little Bitch!

She's going to wind up owing this company. God only knows what she'll achieve. The way she's going, Doris Lehman could wind up humping her way into Forbes magazine.

> *The play's the thing*
> *Wherein I'll catch the conscience of the King.*
> William Shakespeare. Hamlet, II:2

FRAN

Fran finds her position as the writer of a love lorn column a dissatisfying experience, one which negatively affects her personal relationships.

(Reading from a letter.) "Dear Ms. Lonely Hearts: My boyfriend has suddenly started paying a lot of attention to my younger sister. And last evening she told me that he has been making advances toward her. She said that..." *(Dropping the letter.)* Christ! I don't think I can take another one of these. I'm stressed-out, I'm over-problemed, I need a good long vacation. Anyway, who am I to be advising anybody, for Pete's sake? *(Beat for listening.)* So I'm good at it, so what? I'm tired of it, fed up, I've had it. Anyway, it's a stupid job. Five years ago, when they asked me to fill in for a few weeks, I had no idea what I was getting into. Then the thing caught on, mushroomed. Now it's the most popular feature in the paper.

What gets to you is that people actually take your advice seriously, follow it. You realize the power I've got? It's scary. Hey, I'm not qualified to give this kind of advice, not in any academic way. Hell, I'm not degreed, or anything. I'm just a journalism major who got lucky. And the irony of it is, I can't get my own life together. Who the hell do *I* write

20

to? That's the question. Hell, I haven't had a decent relationship since I started writing this crazy column. I have a strong feeling that's my problem; dealing with other people's hang-ups six days a week; with divorce, infidelity, lust — you name it. Anything emotionally untoward I'm into up to my deadlines.

Something tells me so long as I'm "Ms. Lonely Hearts" I'll never have a normal relationship. *(She takes up the letter again and reflects on it.)* Maybe I'll advise this woman to involve herself in a hot *manage a trois* with her boyfriend and sister. A few columns like that and I'll be happily back on the editorial desk in no time.

I saw it at a disadvantage — the curtain was up.
Walter Winchell (1879-1972) US Journalist.

21

ELAINE

A recent negative experience with an over-zealous sports enthusiast has left Elaine angry, disgruntled and decidedly worse for wear.

And then we went jogging. And then we went for racquetball. And then we went for a swim. And then we went for a bike ride. And then — then I went for a chiropractor.

The guy's a sports nut, a freak. And who needs it? All these games and jumping around and straining all the time. And who needs being involved on a competitive level with her date? Like tennis. I mean, alright, a nice friendly little game I can handle, okay? But that's not for this jock-head. He's out for blood. Like we go out to "hit a few" okay? But when we get out there it's all of a sudden Wimbledon and he's out to capture the fucking finals. So I get these ninety-mile-an-hour serves that I can't even see coming that bounce up and smack me in the arms, legs, you name it. I have these big red spots over 70% of my body. Jerk!

And get this. Last Saturday we go to this little tavern over on the the north side and we get into a game of darts. A nice little harmless game played by friendly people who like to have a few and goof-off, right? But nooooo, not for this aggressive son of a bitch.

22

Bev, I've never seen anything like it. Like he was throwing his darts so hard they were going through the board and sticking in the plaster.

And then comes the bike ride which was like a leg of the triathlon. Thirty-five miles. Hey, for this kind of distance you take a cab. And then the jogging. All uphill because he said it was good for your cardiovascular whatever. It was a killer. But not for this drip. He was eating it up, running along wild-eyed in his cool body suit and far-out head band.

Bev, if you ever, and I mean *ever*, fix me up with another guy with a football for a brain, so help me I'll strangle you. Ooooh! Ouch! Lemme me sit down, Quick!

FRANCINE

She considers cosmetic surgery.

I didn't used to think about aging. But lately, it's become more of a thing. Even though I'm not that old, I'm beginning to see these telltale signs creeping in. A little sag here, a bag there, a subtle line, a wrinkle, a crinkle. Especially around my eyes. *(She probes gently under her eyes.)* Do you think I'm starting to bag-out? *(Beat.)* You sure? I don't know. I think maybe I should go for an eye job. The only trouble is, it costs a fortune. These surgeons don't work cheap. I checked one out last week — Dr. Wolf in the new medical complex. He's noted for his eye work. Dr. Foreman's the best for chins, Dr. Friedman's tops when it comes to lifts and tucks. These guys all have their specialities.

Anyway, Wolf — he's a doll, by the way, you should see him — Wolf tells me I'm a good candidate for an eye job, that all I have is this disease that causes this puffiness. Very common, he says. He showed me some before and after pictures of his patients and the changes were dramatic. He does noses, too. But I understand Dr. Weinberger does the best nose jobs. He doesn't take off so much you wind up looking like a Pekinese. Ida Gross had Weinberger do her nose and she looks terrific. She used to look like the Wicked Witch of the West, remember?

I still haven't made up my mind. I asked Milt what he thought and he said he liked me the way I am, that my eyes look okay to him. That's Milt for you. He isn't exactly your aesthetic type person. Like when we visited the Grand Canyon he never left the hotel. He stayed inside the whole time and played computer games.

I think maybe I'll go for the eye job. It'll take off ten years. *(Beat.)* You think my nose is too big?

It was the kind of show where the girls are not autitioned — just measured.
Irene Thomas (1920-) British writer.

ESTHER

A trouper, from a long line of show folk, has little patience with the artiste.

We do two shows a day, three on Saturday. We work. We just *do* it. We don't stand around looking for motivation and attempt to be arty farty. We're pros who get out there and knock ourselves out and do our best to give people their money's worth. And, sometimes, it isn't easy; sometimes it's damned hard to get up for it because you've done the show a million times. But, like I said — we do it.

There are a lot of actors around who have deluded themselves into believing they're this special package set down on earth by divine grace, or something, that their profession gives them an excuse to behave strangely. Nonsense! Acting, the arts, all of it, is just another profession, another choice. All of this introspective, intellectual garbage about the "body" of someone's work, for example, and about methods and motivations is nothing but twenty tons of pure, unadulterated nonsense spread in fifty directions.

You show me an artist who takes himself seriously and I'll show you stilted work and a person who has a nutritionist, changes religion once a week, breaks for sunbeams and who, generally, has his Zen head up his ying-yang. Me, my family, we're troupers.

26

We get out there and bust our buns to give people what they've paid for — entertainment. We're entertainers.

And now we win this award and all of a sudden we discover we're "creative artists." And I guess we are, at that. We're very much aware of "creating" a decent performance and "creating" a decent paycheck. One reviewer recently said this about us: "They are sensitive purveyors of the thespian art." With all due respects, excuse me, but I may get sick.

The Great White Way. Albert Bigelow Paine. (1861-1937) US writer. From his book title.

ADA

She speaks with great affection of her true love, Will.

I first met Will the night 'e come up from Charleston. He'd been a drivin' all night an' 'e looked like the slum-side a hell. Looked about the same as 'e does t'day — skinny devil with no teeth. But 'e was sure cute. Anyway, I sure thought 'e was. He had this here way about 'im. Man could charm the livin' daylights outta a woman, still can. Anyway, 'e sure got on through t' me, gums an' all. A woman don't notice the uglies when a man's got himself some character; when 'e's got a holt on soul and can spill it out and show it and let it take over ever'thin' around 'im; when 'e's got it big and huge an' can blow it up an' make it bigger an' bigger.

Well, it was a rainy night, I remember, a kinda drizlin' behind a bone-cold wind. I was settin' here, right at this here table, a workin' on a double Southern Comfort when Will slid in a lookin' like a ruptured pup. His old Dodge had busted on 'im up near Floyd Mear's place and the crazy rascal had walked all the way in. He went on over t' the bar there an' ordered 'imself a shot and 'e looked real interestin' standin' there in the light from the Miller's sign. That there red neon on that there crazy face was like sunrise on Mount Rushmore, it lit 'im up t' real advantage. Anyway, 'e looked real

28

okay t' me. I've always liked men who look like they bin in pain fer a few days.

He couldn't help but notice me a settin' here, so 'e come on over and set down an' bought me another Comfort and we started in t' talkin', him an' me, a talkin', a spinnin' a little history an' a lot a lies an' a gettin' real chummy an' I felt m'self a driftin' inta 'is slow-freight charm. I say slow-freight 'cause 'e was a comin' at me steady with a heavy load.

Well sir, that there started up the beginnin' of it, an' me an' Will's bin talkin' real chummy ever since. An, Alice, honey, ya know, I still git me a thrill when I see that there skinny devil a comin' at me from across a room.

Tallulah Bankhead barged down the Nile last night and sank. As the Serpent of the Nile she proves to be no more dangerous than a garter snake. John Mason Brown (1900-1969) US critic. Referring to her performance as Shakespeare's Cleopatra.

DRAMA

KIMBERLY

Kimberly, paralyzed from the chest down, recalls the tragic incident causing her impairment.

We'd gone to see a movie, Carol and I, and after the picture we were walking along window shopping when suddenly this car comes from out of nowhere. It was on me in a second.

I remember seeing headlights and this oncoming windshield and I remember tumbling over the car and down its trunk and into a news stand. It all happened so quickly. I learned later that I'd been carried along for over a hundred feet.

They rushed me to the hospital. My lungs were bruised and my brain was damaged which left me with a learning difficulty and one eye that wouldn't dilate, and paralyzed. I was given a 10% chance of surviving. But I made it. They say I'm a miracle.

I'm still in therapy, working every day to rehabilitate and get back to living. My friends have been wonderful and supportive and loving. Without them I don't think I could have made it.

The memory of the incident is still with me, still a vivid nightmare. And then there's the tragedy of what happened to some of other pedestrians. Horrible. One little boy was killed outright.

The man who ran us down was arrested and charged with murder and with 48 counts of attempted murder and assault.

At first I didn't think I'd be able cope with being paralyzed. I was so damned resentful. Why me? I hated life, everybody, everything. But now, now slowly, I'm coming out of it, I'm getting myself together. I'm realizing that there are still things I can do, things worth living for. I can still be useful and contribute. Of course, things won't be normal. But I still have a life and I'm going to use it. Believe it or not, I'm actually looking forward to so many things.

There is less in this than meets the eye. Tallulah Bankhead (1903-1968). Referring to a play by Maeterlinck.

LISA

Lisa speaks before her chapter of AA.

I started drinking about seven years ago. Casually, at first — beer and wine. Harmless enough, I thought. At least it seemed so at the time. I mean, I was having fun, so...why not, okay?

The habit seemed to kind of creep up on me, little by little, subtly. Till it finally it took over, and took hold of my life. My first indication I had a problem was when I'd drink and it was no longer enjoyable and left me feeling flat and depressed. By then, though, I needed it, had to have it — I was hooked. At first, I thought I could shake it. But I just couldn't. I tried, but I couldn't. Every time I made a commitment to quit I broke it.

I was slipping more and more into the alcoholic pattern: reckless behavior, car wrecks, trouble with relationships, murderous hangovers, waking up in strange beds. And my job was going to hell. Then there were the overpowering feelings of remorse and hating myself and all that. And it became like this cycle, you know? winding down tighter and tighter until I was on the bottom, constantly depressed, feeling worthless and afraid.

Then finally, thank God, I called AA. I finally got up the nerve to face up, to come to grips with my problem. And that was the turning point; that's when I started coming back, regaining my self-respect.

It's been nearly a year since I've had a drink. A year this next Tuesday, to be exact. I'm making it. By God I'm making it — one day at a time.

I have knocked everything but the knees of the chorus giris. Nature anticipated us there.
Percy Hammond (1873-1936) US drama critic.

DALE

Dale, a rape victim, relives the horror, tells of the residual pain and humiliation.

Please! Stop! You have no idea. None. Nobody does until they've gone through it. It's not something you shrug off overnight; it's not something you set aside like a book you've just finished reading. There are scars. Believe me, there are scars. The residue of it is like a cancer, something that's malignant and ugly and threatening.

Even though it's been almost a year now, I still have nightmares. I still shiver with fear, remembering, reliving that night and the terror of it, the way he sprang from the back seat of my car and overpowered me. And then...then there was the trial which seemed to drag on forever, resulting in the son of a bitch getting off and waltzing out of the courtroom with this look of smug defiance.

In many ways, the trial was the worst of it. The ordeal of it, going over the details, confronting this arrogant animal. And then there was the way people related to me. Friends, people I'd known for years, suddenly shyed away from me like I was, was this leper, or something. And here I was the victim. The victim! But they made me feel like I was the perpetrator. Then, there were the insidious goddamn rumors. Comments like: "She had it coming," "She asked for it." Christ! I was the *victim!* I was the victim of this brutal act and I went home in the evenings feeling like a murderer. And Robert? Well, that was the end of us. The beginning of the end, anyway. He couldn't handle it, the fact I was "spoiled goods."

No, you haven't any idea. You can't have. Nobody can but the woman.

There's No Business Like Show Business.
Irving Berlin (1888-1989).

RACHEL

Rachel, a victim of sexual harassment in the work place, is understandably acrimonious.

Men have their pressures, no doubt. But it's different for a man. They don't have to cope with some fool pushing himself on them, using sex as a weapon, as a means of controlling them and threatening their security.

I've had to work hard to get where I am; into a responsible position where I'm making respectable money; the same money a man gets for a comparable job. And now the pressure's *really* on.

Wilson knows I'm up for another promotion and he also knows he holds the key to it, that my advancement has to come from his recommendation. So, what's he doing? He's compromising me. Day after day there's the innuendo, the inane, sickening little remarks. And when I rebuff him he recoils like a hurt worm and tells me to be nice. Sure, and we all know what "nice" means. It means becoming a service station for some slimeball. And then, afterwards, it means you become hot news for the corporate gossip mill because men like Harry talk because sex means conquest for them and all the stilted-brained assholes like them who are ten percent man and ninety percent ego.*(Beat.)* It's isn't easy.

LAURA

Laura recalls brutality at the hands of a drunken father.

We lived in this little apartment in Pittsburgh. A dingy, cramped place. Dad was a steel worker at J&L — a tough job. Maybe it was the work that got to him, I don't know. All I know is he was never kind, not really. The only time he showed any affection was after he'd beaten me, when he was sober and feeling guilty. *(Beat.)* I remember how he'd come home drunk, bouncing off the walls. He was madman — screaming at Mother, making demands, swearing, forcing her to have sex with him right there in front of me. Then he'd turn on me. He'd slap me and pound me and shove me and drag me by my hair. And for nothing, for no apparent reason. Or maybe for my honest reactions — I hated him and I let him know it.

I didn't have a childhood, I had a hell. Hell like you can't imagine unless you've lived it. Mother and I were nothing more than an outlet for is anger and frustrations. We were victims of his meanness and hostility. And I've never gotten over it. It's stayed with me and affected me and my attitude toward men. I still carry the psychological damage because I had a father who gave me brutality instead of love.

40

JULIE

Julie remonstrates regarding her lesbianism during this parental confrontation.

You've really never accepted it, have you, Mother? You, the family, any of you. Not really. You're still so ashamed. It's so glaringly obvious in your attitudes.

And how do you think it makes me feel? And Sandi? You think she can't tell, doesn't feel ill at ease because of your condescending manners, your devastating side-long glances, your sweet smugness, your "I guess we'll just have to grin and bear it," attitudes? Please, Mother, please don't do us any favors!

Is it so terrible to love another woman, Mother? Is it? Does it make me some kind of far-out freak, or something? Is this something so new, so terrible, so sinful — lesbianism? *(Beat.)* Yes, I suppose it is for this family, for my wonderful family. It squares with all you've ever heard and imagined about the evilness of "queers"" and "homos."

You're all so damned threatened, it seems, so weak — like your religion. If your faith was valid it would have room for growth and enlightenment,

41

wouldn't it, instead of having to protect itself through fear?

You're all so terribly, terribly afraid. Afraid of truth, afraid of feelings. You're all so hopelessly, terribly goddamned afraid! And you know what? I pity you. Yes, I pity you, I really do. Because you're all so narrow-minded and unbelievably small and because your prejudices shut out love.

Popular stage-plays are sinful, heathenish, lewd, ungodly Spectacles and most pernicious Corruptions, condemned in all ages as intolerable Mischiefs to Churches, to Republics, to the manners, minds and souls of men. William Prine (1600-1669) English Puritan.

JOSLYN

Joslyn justifies daydreaming.

Every now and then I think it's very healthy to get into the dream world.

I've been a daydreamer since I was a child. I was always drifting off in school, gazing off into space, spinning fantasies. I was this demon weaver of mental abstractions. I created mental patterns, you might say. And I still do. I'm still a dream weaver.

In "The Summing Up" Somerset Maughm gave a lot of weight to patterns. Like how a each life is like an oriental rug and has a very definite, unique design and how an ordered life follows the pattern and how a disordered one deviates from it and is thrown into chaos. As I see it, daydreams have logical shapes also.

And day dreaming lets me escape, too, lets me fly. And I find it a very creative thing. And Valid. Valid because it unlocks me and relaxes me. People are so grounded, don't you think? Their schematic is soldered for life and, unfortunately, they'll never ever experience a nice healthy short circuit. Too bad.

When I was younger I used to get a lot of heat about daydreaming. My parents, my teachers would come down on me for drifting. And I can understand their concern. I mean, if you're locked in this far-out state all the time, obviously you've got a problem. But what I'm talking about here is the ability to let the mind go as means of getting in touch with the endless possibilities of the imagination. Writers and painters, for instance, they dream on paper and canvasses. Like it's part of their process, you know? The same thing with actors, too, they use their imaginations to create believable characters. I hope this all makes sense. Well, it does to me, anyhow.

Today I'm really stressed-out. So do you know what I'm going to do come lunch time? I'm going over to the park and daydream like crazy.

Two things should be cut: the second act and the child's throat. Noel Coward (1899-1973). Referring to a play featuring a child actor.

CLAUDIA

Claudia, a young, but seasoned politician, is far from naive regarding the reasons for her being asked to share the ticket.

You say you want me on the ticket, right? Okay, I buy it. But not because you *want* me on the ticket. Huh uh. You don't want me on the ticket — you *need* me on this ticket, mister.

You know damned well the only way you're going to win this thing is to run with a woman. Your constituency's demanding it. You think I haven't seen the polls? With me as your running mate, you've got a good chance. So don't patronize me with "wanting" me, please! If anything, you'd love to have me out of your shit because I'm a threat. Because I'm able, informed, and in touch with the people and their problems and needs. You'd rather have some hack running mate you can bury after the elections; some guy who'll stand by and turn his head to your incompetence. *Want* me? What a laugh! *(Pause.)*

Please! Let me finish. *(Beat.)* I've been around. Even though I'm young, I've been there. Up from the roots, involved in the backbiting, the deals, the smears and corruption. I know the cold facts of politics. You need a woman on this ticket and you need her desperately and you've going to get her because — I accept! And certainly not because I respect you. No. Quite the contrary. Frankly, I think you're a lightweight. That's one of the reasons I'm accepting — as a fail-safe against you trashing the office. That and the fact, as a woman, I've got an obligation to the gender, an obligation to get more women into positions of responsibility.

Where you made your first mistake was announcing that you wanted me. Now you're going to have me whether you want me or not. I'm in, honey — for the ride, the duration, whatever. So, call in the press. We don't want to keep the darlings waiting, do we?

When you get the personality, you don't need the nudity. Mae West (1892-1980).

LYNN

A tough, courageous lady, lays it on the line to a small-town racketeer.

Why, you bastard! You with your inflated arrogance and small mind. You're nothing gut a conniving, manipulative son of a bitch who uses your muscle to make life unbearable for pour, weak, miserable slobs.

When I first came to this town all I ever heard was what a great man Frank Eli was; what a big man he was and what power he had. I heard you were really something. Well, they were right about that, you're something, alright, something disgusting and low. And you don't have power. Not anymore. All you have is what's left of a two-bit, past tense operation that's all over. All over because *you're* all over because of your greed and dishonesty. The people are wise to you and how destructive you've been and how you've bled the community all these years without ever giving anything back. They know you're a no good fucking leach bastard. You're over, man, history — finished! Why, in six months nobody'll even remember your name. "Frank who? Oh, yeah, you mean the slimeball who used to run numbers and cheap hookers over on the island. The corrupt bastard who got shut down and run out of town because he thought he was God." It's all over Frankie. You just died!

PAULA

Paula, a waitress, speaks of the time when hopes for a successful acting career were a consuming, driving passion.

I was going to be famous. And rich, or course. Anyway, that's what I'd promised myself. I think a lot of us set goals like that when everything is new and untarnished. But as time wears on, and the years slip into history, you learn to settle for less, lower your expectations for ruling the world. I mean, there are realities. When I came to work here the idea was for it to be a temporary thing. Kind of a stop over on my way to stardom.

At first, for a long time, I didn't take the job seriously. I fluffed it, you know? My mind wasn't in it. I don't know how they put up with me. I was lazy and flip and a terrible waitress.

On my days off I'd go around to agents and casting directors and production companies trying to make connections and pick up acting work. I was in a little theatre group, a workshop, you name it. Every now and then I'd get work in a feature or TV. Nothing big, just in a background shot or a group or maybe I'd have a line or two. Just enough to keep me going because people would see me and compliment me and tell me I was this great type. But the jobs were few and far between. Most of the time — nothing. After

48

a few years of living on the edge and hearing a lot of false flattery and phony promises I began to tire of it. It was a hopeless, frustrating life.

Little by little I began to settle in here. Started to get more into the job, got to be a better waitress, more professional. Now, I'm the best here, the best paid, I make the biggest tips. I do alright. And I like the job and the people. Especially my old customers. It's like they're family. Occasionally, though, I wonder if I could have made it. I was a great looking girl. And I had talent, I think. Who knows?

Would either of you like desert?

> *She's not going to walk in here...and turn it into a Golden Sanitary Towel Award Presentation.*
> John Osborne.

49

NANCY

Nancy recalls the passing of her father.

I was there at the end.   I'd never seen anyone die
before.   I've always avoided such things.   But...I
mean...when it's your parent you can't run from it.

I hadn't seen Dad in awhile.   In over two years.   I
should have gone home more often.   I knew he'd
been having stomach pains.   Mother told me.   And
in his photos he looked bloated and strange.   He was
being eaten alive by cancer.   But they thought, he and
mother that is, they thought is was just poor diet and
gastritis and that.   And he refused to go to the doctor
— he hated them.

Finally, a little over a month ago, he just couldn't
stand the pain any longer and Mom talked him into
going in for a checkup.   Well, the X-rays showed a
dark spot near his diaphragm and they recommended
an exploratory operation right away.   When they
opened him up they found the cancer.   They gave
him six months.   He was never told.   Mother decided
not to.

They were planning to move out here and rent a
place so we could be all together.   Then, suddenly,
Mother called and told me to come home right away.

When I got there he was near the end. I was shocked at the sight of him. He was terribly thin and emaciated. It was frightful.

He passed away quietly within a few days. I was numb, and at the funeral I was just going through the motions, I didn't know where I was. Frankly, I found the whole funeral thing to be a cold, business-like ritual. I mean, what the hell, here we were dealing with...I mean...Christ! the man'd been my father! The thought of never seening him again was just —

I just wish we'd been closer, that all. There were so many feelings we never shared.

> *I was born at the age of twelve on the Metro-Goldwyn-Mayer lot.* Judy Garland (Frances Gumm; 1922-1969).

DALE

Dale reveals her affection for her recently departed pet.

I guess I'm not as sophisticated as I thought I was. Here I am, a woman with a Masters in psychology, and I'm all torn up over losing a mangy old tom cat.

But, he was company — a good friend. He was quietly understanding when I rambled on to him regarding my problems. He was a neat old cat, a noble creature. Cats are, you know? They're most noble and resiliently independent — and loving without being servile.

My neighbors came over and told me last evening. They'd found Midnight in a hedge near the house. He'd obviously been struck by a car. I was devastated.

You know, I never realized how much emotion was running between me and that animal. Over the years a person develops a tremendously warm and loving relationship with his pet.

I've never been an outgoing, gregarious person, not really. I generally tend to shy away from people, social situations. Maybe it's because I deal with troubled people all day long. Perhaps. But I've always been a loner. People have never been my

52

long suit. I mean, on a truly intimate level in relation to my real feelings and emotions and problems, that is. I can usually see into the problems of others, can advise and consul, but when it comes to my own hang-ups —

Midnight filled a great void. He was like having another person in the house, something living I could talk to and pour out my feelings to. It was as though that old cat really listened, understood. I confided more personal information to Midnight than any other living thing.

I'm going to miss Midnight, his low purring, his hopping up onto my bed at night, the warmth of his body next to mine.

I really loved that mangy old tom.

Hollywood is a world with all the personality of a paper cup. Raymond Chandler (1888-1959).

ABBY

Abby's days of marijuana and alcohol addiction are still painfully vivid.

I didn't use anything at all in high school. In fact, I was dead set against it. I saw what happened to the kids who became strung-out; saw them go from bright, thinking individuals to lethargic, unmotivated blobs. Here they were, these young kids, with no life in their eyes, living from drink to drink, from hit to hit. The transformation was stark. Here would be this nice looking kid, from a good home, with everything going for him, here he'd be just going through the motions with this deadly attitude of disinterest and hopelessness. Sad. Really sad.

I did my first dope during my junior year in college. Was just this offhand experience, you know? A couple of the girls in my dorm were doing drugs and dealing, so stuff was available. Maybe it was the pressure. I was studying pre-law and carrying a pretty heavy load and — no! that's bullshit! I can't make excuses for it. The stuff was there and I went for it, started experimenting and getting heavier into the scene. Before I knew it I was addicted to grass, hooked, I needed it to function.

I got to the point where I was out of it most of the time, not really caring much about anything. Days came and went. I became this immoblized zombie just like the kids I'd known in high school. But I didn't realize it at the time. You don't. You don't have an honest perspective on just how messed up you really are. It usually takes some drastic happening to put you in touch with the state of your deterioration.

Piling up my car was the turning point. Realizing what I'd done and how close I'd come to becoming history snapped me back and I started to regain control of my life. I was lucky. Some never pull out; they just keep going down further and further until they become hopelessly addicted and kill themselves or somebody else. Like I said — I was lucky.

> *It was like going to the dentist making a picture with her. It was hell at the time, but after it was all over, it was wonderful.* Billy Wilder (1906-). Referring to Marylin Monroe.

JENNIFER

Jennifer, a writer, speaks of her roots, its impact upon her work.

Our home was a beautiful place. I have such fond, vivid memories of it. It was a great old farm house that represented this bastion of clarity against the madness of the convoluted world. It holds a special place in my past and heart — a place like none other.

It was a large, brick house with walls a foot thick and a working fireplace in each room; fireplaces that were always burning during the colder months, keeping us cozy, insulating us from the elements, the capriciousness of the midwestern winters. In that rock-solid old farm house we were safe and secure. No harm could befall us there. Not in that great, red brick womb.

I have wonderful memories of the old homestead, of my mother and father and grandparents, my brothers and sisters. My, how happy we were during those long ago, simplistic times.

I've drawn upon those times repeatedly for my novels, using them as background to humanize and color my stories. As a writer, I'm very fortunate to have been involved in such a rich tapestry. It has helped my career immeasurably. But this is only one of the many ways I'm enriched by the memories. Perhaps the most important thing I've retained from those days of farm life is a feeling for the inexorable cycle that confronted me there. You were forced to witness birth and growing and death. You were part of that; part of the cyclical, seasonal realities — the cycle of life.

Hollywood — a place where people from Iowa mistake themselves for movie stars.
Fred Allen (1894-1956) American comedian.

DONNA

Donna unfolds the pitfalls of seeing a married man.

There was never any secret. I knew from the first he was a married man. So, I can't blame him. And, at first, it worked out okay. I'd made up my mind to accept the fact there was no future. But as time went on and I fell more and more in love it became harder and harder to accept the fact that it was a hopeless situation.

In the beginning you sell yourself on the realities. I mean, you're an adult, you're going into this thing with your eyes wide open, right? All that sounds good at first, you buy all the cliche's. But where there are really deep feelings involved...well...you can't intellectualize when it comes to feelings.

We met once a week. At my apartment. We never had weekends together, that was understood from the first. His weekends were reserved for his family. Initally all this was okay, but, after awhile, I wanted more of him and I began resenting him being with another woman, a woman who obviously had a hold on him and he respected.

Little by little, I grew to resent him — the whole situation. Even though I loved him I started to grow angry deep down inside. And, after awhile, that anger begins to eat away at you and it takes over and things are said which lead to arguments and uglies. And even though you make up, there is this residual anger that continues to undercut and there are lingering resentments and psychological reprisals. And once this happens, it's the beginning of the end.

I haven't seen Dave in over six months. And I still love him. Maybe I always will. But the whole thing was a lie, false. A woman needs her self-respect, needs hope and something solid and love that's free and open. And besides, there's something just plain sick about being involved with another woman's man.

Photography is truth. And cinema is truth twenty-four times a second. Jean-Luc Godard (1930-)French film director.

This non-objective speech is presented in the interest of variety. Ordinary construction has ben avoided in the interest of free interpretation. The stress here is laid on word-play rather than the substantive. Bend this speech, allow any images evoked by it to fire your emotions.

Dog barks open many doors. These dog barks will be remembered for their darkness, for limitless removal. Forty dogs straddle a window pane. Forty window panes straddled by creatures woofing in a room. Room run run done boom boom! The room is a cymbal crash. The window is a bass drum. Forty dogs are nothing. But can this nothing be nothing? For to recognize it is to give it substance and meaning. Don't listen to what I'm saying. Lend me you silence, give me your other selves. Elaborate and spin. Work and toil and sit a while and forgive. Forgive these dogs, all forty, these forty without homes and little bones and major inconveniences. They must pay. They must strive and they must bark. Woofy woof woof! Bark! Where? What? Was it a dalmatian? A huskie? Ah! Limitless possibilities unfold here if you are not listening. Please don't listen. Stop listening! Close your minds and understand. Destroy all major works and lesser works and middle ground efforts. This is the dogs way. Forty dogs on a still night in Dayton, Ohio. Are they still there? Are they still waiting? Bless these canines. They are you and me.